The SPORTS CLUB

Basketball

Matt Parselle

PRINCETON ■ LONDON

Published in the United States and Canada by
Two-Can Publishing LLC
234 Nassau Street
Princeton, NJ 08542

www.two-canpublishing.com

© 2000, 1999 Two-Can Publishing

For information on Two-Can books and multimedia, call
1-609-921-6700, fax 1-609-921-3349, or visit our Web site at
http://www.two-canpublishing.com

Created by
act-two
346 Old Street
London EC1V 9RB

Text: Matt Parselle
Editor: Lucy Arnold
Senior editor: Jacqueline McCann
Senior designer: Helen McDonagh
Art director: Belinda Webster
Consultant: Graham Jones, EBBA Regional
  Development Manager, South and South-west
Computer generated figures: Jonatronix
Computer illustrations: Mel Pickering
Picture research: Jenny West
Pre-press production: Adam Wilde

'Two-Can' is a trademark of Two-Can Publishing.
Two-Can Publishing is a division of Zenith Entertainment plc,
43-45 Dorset Street, London W1H 4AB.

HC ISBN 1-58728-0000
SC ISBN 1-58728-0027

HC 1 2 3 4 5 6 7 8 9 10 02 01 00
SC 1 2 3 4 5 6 7 8 9 10 02 01 00

Photographic credits: Allsport p5, p8, p12, p17, p18, p19,
p20, p22, p24, p25, p26, p27, p28 (left), p29 (top left & bottom);
Colorsport p9, p23; Empics p10, p14, p16; Image Bank p11;
NBA Photos p28 (right), p29 (top right)

Front cover: Allsport (top left & top right); Action Plus (bottom)
Back cover: Allsport

Printed in Hong Kong by Wing King Tong

Contents

94877

Words in **bold** in the text are explained here, along with other useful basketball terms.

Getting started

Backboards are made of wood, tough plastic or safety glass.

" Welcome to the fast and exciting world of basketball! I'm your coach and I'm here to set you off on the right track. There are several different ways of playing basketball – in this book we follow **US college** rules. Ready? Let's begin! "

For a game, the basket is 10 feet off the ground.

What you need

You don't need any fancy equipment to play basketball. That's why it's so popular! If you can practice with a friend, that's great, but there are lots of skills you can learn on your own, too. So if you have a basket and a ball, you're ready to train.

HOT TIPS
If you don't have a basket, practice **shooting** against a brick wall. Aim for the same brick on the wall every time.

BASKETBALL GEAR

1 When you practice, wear loose-fitting clothes so that you can move around easily.

2 When you play a game, you and your teammates should wear the same color shorts and shirt, called your uniform.

3 A basketball shirt has a number on the front and the back. Each player on a team chooses a different number. Why not pick the same number as your favorite player?

Basketballs come in different sizes. Most college players use a ball that is about 29 inches in circumference.

Wear basketball shoes that support your ankles, cushion your feet and give you a good grip on the **court**.

Keep your fingernails short so that you don't hurt other players.

Thick socks help to keep your feet comfortable.

Warming up

It's essential to warm up before a game – otherwise you might pull a muscle. Skip or jog up and down the court for a few minutes. Then try these exercises to stretch your leg muscles.

1 First, stretch the inside of your leg. Squat down, keeping your left leg as straight as possible. Count to ten, then try your right leg.

2 To stretch your calf muscles, lean against a wall. Keep your right leg straight behind you and your feet flat on the floor. Count to ten, then change legs.

Ball practice

Before you start playing, practice bouncing the ball. Drop the ball from shoulder-height onto a smooth, flat surface. The ball should bounce up to between your waist and chest. Off you go...

1 First, try bouncing the ball with both hands together. Keep your eyes on the ball.

2 When you've mastered that, use just one hand. Try lifting your head and looking straight ahead.

Team talk

Basketball is a team game. Good team spirit will help you play well and enjoy yourself at the same time. Learn the tactics in this book and you'll be able to play a great team game with your friends.

▶ Practicing with friends will help you to improve your ball-control skills.

Meet the team

Lucy

Rob

" A basketball team has five players and you can play in one of three positions – **guard**, **center** or **forward**. Whichever position you choose, you'll need to master all the skills of the game. It's time to meet the members of the team and find out more... "

Guards

Our job is to move the ball down the court toward the basket, so we need to be good at **dribbling** and passing the ball. It also helps if we're quick on our feet.

Team formation

Any player can move anywhere on the **court**. In defense, the coach may use a pattern, or **zone** to keep the players spread out. The simplest pattern has two guards, one center and two forwards, so it's known as the 2-1-2 zone. A coach may use more centers to make his team more attacking, or more guards for a stronger defense.

▶ Here is our team in their **front court** – that's the half of the court they're attacking. The coach has arranged the team in a 2-1-2 zone so that all of the front court is well covered.

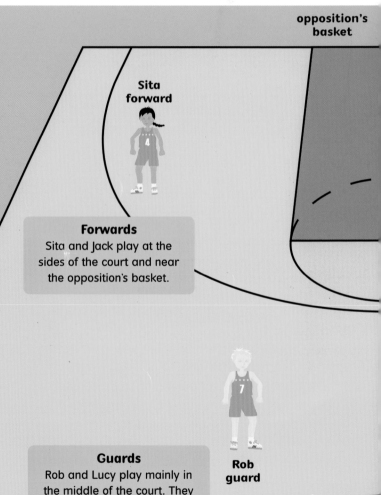

opposition's basket

Sita
forward

Forwards
Sita and Jack play at the sides of the court and near the opposition's basket.

The red team is playing toward the opposition's basket.

Guards
Rob and Lucy play mainly in the middle of the court. They are the nearest players to their own basket.

Rob
guard

Sita

Jack

HOT TIPS
Don't worry if you're not sure which position you want to play. Once you've learned all the skills, then you can decide.

Adam

Forwards

Forwards score mainly from the sides of the court. When the ball **rebounds**, or bounces, off the **backboard**, we try to reach the ball first and **shoot** again.

Center

I'm usually the tallest player in the team. I make sure the ball goes into the basket, by shooting from close range and by scoring from rebounds.

**Adam
center**

**Jack
forward**

Center
Adam plays in the middle of the court and near the opposition's basket.

Coach and substitutes
The coach and team substitutes sit on the team bench. When the coach wants to change his strategy, he may bring on a substitute to replace one of the players.

Table officials
Officials who keep score and record the time sit at the scorer's table.

**Lucy
guard**

Referee and umpire
A **referee** and an umpire watch the game to make sure the teams play by the rules.

7

Game play

" Hi, I'm the **referee**, or the Ref, and I'm in charge of the game. Other officials help me keep track of the score and the time. A **college game** usually lasts for 40 minutes, and all the action takes place on a **court**. Let's take a look... **"**

▲ During a game, officials make hand signals to each other. This signal means that a player has committed a **foul**.

The court

A basketball court is marked out on a flat surface, usually made of wood. Official courts have digital clocks and electronic scoreboards, but don't worry, all you really need for a game is a court and two baskets!

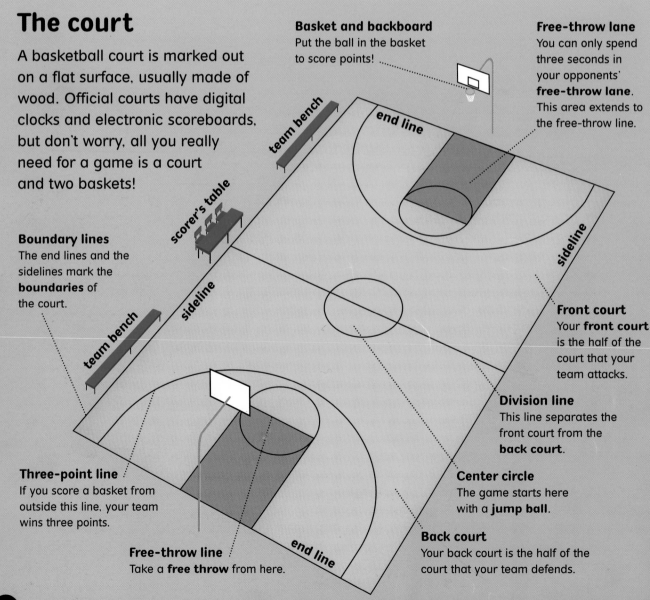

Basket and backboard
Put the ball in the basket to score points!

Free-throw lane
You can only spend three seconds in your opponents' **free-throw lane**. This area extends to the free-throw line.

team bench

end line

scorer's table

sideline

Boundary lines
The end lines and the sidelines mark the **boundaries** of the court.

team bench

sideline

Front court
Your **front court** is the half of the court that your team attacks.

Division line
This line separates the front court from the **back court**.

Three-point line
If you score a basket from outside this line, your team wins three points.

Free-throw line
Take a **free throw** from here.

end line

Center circle
The game starts here with a **jump ball**.

Back court
Your back court is the half of the court that your team defends.

Scoring

The team that scores the most points wins the game. The only way to collect points is by scoring goals, or baskets, so start **shooting**! The number of points you win for a basket depends on where you were standing when you shot the ball. Here's how it works...

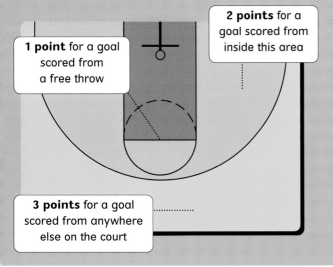

1 point for a goal scored from a free throw

2 points for a goal scored from inside this area

3 points for a goal scored from anywhere else on the court

▲ An **NBA** game takes place in a huge arena. A scoreboard hangs over the court to make sure all the spectators know what's going on.

Jump ball

A game begins with a jump ball. One player from each team stands in the center circle and the Ref throws the ball high into the air between them. During the game, if the Ref can't decide which team should have the ball, he gives a jump ball in the nearest circle.

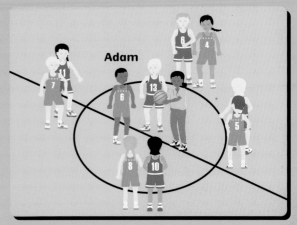

Adam

❶ Here is the red team at the start of a game. Adam is in his back court, next to his opponent. The other players must be standing outside the center circle when the Ref throws the ball.

❷ Once the ball has reached its highest point in the air, the two players jump up and try to tap the ball to a teammate.

DON'T FORGET
During a game, you're not allowed to carry, or deliberately kick or punch, the ball.

Game rules

❝ Basketball is all about fast action and fair play, so there are a few rules to remember. If you unfairly hinder another player, it's called a **foul**. If you break any other rule, it's a **violation** and I give the ball to the other team. **❞**

▲ Toni Kukoc receives the ball. Kukoc is Croatia's biggest star and he plays in the **NBA** for the Chicago Bulls.

Throw-in

When the **Ref** tells you to take a throw-in, stand **out-of-bounds**, which means just outside the **boundary lines** of the court. Make sure you keep both feet behind the line as you throw the ball onto the court.

Rob takes a throw-in. Adam moves free of his opponent and signals for the ball.

Other violations

To stay on the Ref's good side, bear in mind these two other important rules…

When you're defending, never touch the ball when it's dropping down toward the basket. Otherwise, your opponents win points as if the ball had gone in.

Out-of-bounds

Watch your step when you've got the ball and you're near a boundary line. If you touch or cross the line, it's a violation. Try not to knock the ball out-of-bounds either – the Ref will award the ball to the other team.

Lucy is **dribbling** the ball when her foot touches the sideline. She's out-of-bounds, so it's a violation.

sideline

Once the ball is in the **front court**, you must not pass it to anyone in the **back court**. Here, Sita cannot pass to Rob until he has crossed the division line.

Foul

Usually, when you commit a foul, it's a **free throw**, or shot at the basket, from the free-throw line. But if you foul someone who is **shooting**, the Ref will give the shooter up to three free throws. If you commit five fouls, you're off the court, so be careful! Here are the two main types of foul...

A technical foul is given for bad or unsporting behavior, such as arguing with the Ref!

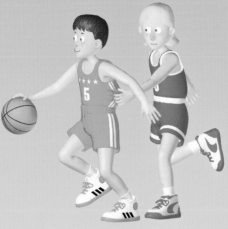

The green player is holding onto Jack to stop him from moving away. This is called a personal foul.

TIME RULES

If your team is too slow when you're attacking, you risk breaking one of these time rules, and that's a violation!

1 Once the ball is put into play, you must shoot within 35 seconds (30 seconds for women).

2 If your team wins the ball in the back court, you must move the ball into the front court before 10 seconds are up (30 seconds for women).

3 If you are holding the ball in the front court and you are closely guarded, you have 5 seconds to advance the ball.

4 You can only spend 3 seconds in your opponents' free-throw lane.

Finally, there are a couple of extra time rules to bear in mind.

1 Each team can take 5 breaks, called time outs, during a game. Teams are also allowed an extra time out for each overtime period.

2 If scores are tied at the end of the game, play continues in five-minute overtime periods until one team wins.

▲ A coach talks tactics with his players during a time out. Here, the coach is drawing the formation he wants the team to use.

Dribbling

❝ There are three ways to move the ball – **dribble**, pass, or **shoot**. I'm going to show you how to dribble – that's bouncing the ball on the floor while you're on the move. But first, we'll take a look at holding the ball. **❞**

▲ John Stockton of Utah Jazz is a brilliant dribbler and passer. See how he keeps his head up as he moves.

The triple threat

You need to know how to position yourself while you're holding the ball, so that you can look around and decide what to do next. The **triple-threat position** gives you a choice of three things to do with the ball: dribble, pass, or shoot. This is how it works...

Sita stands in the triple-threat position. She holds the ball firmly at chest-height, her feet are apart, and she's ready for action.

As Sita considers her three options, she glances around the **court**. She decides to dribble away from her opponent. Nice work, Sita!

Basic dribbling

Dribbling is a great way to move the ball down the court toward the basket. Once you've got the hang of this skill, you'll have the whole game at your fingertips! But don't bounce the ball too high, or you'll give your opponent a chance to sneak in and steal it.

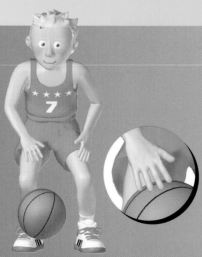

Rob pushes the ball down firmly and smoothly with his fingertips. He keeps his knees bent and his head up.

As the ball bounces back up, Rob spreads his fingers to meet it. He looks straight ahead all the time.

Pivoting

When you've stopped dribbling, you can't start again, so you have to pass the ball or shoot. One thing you can do is **pivot**, or turn around on the spot, either with small steps or in one move, while keeping one foot fixed. This helps you face the way you want to throw the ball.

Jack keeps his left foot on the same spot and turns around, taking small steps with his right foot. He holds the ball close to his chest.

Here, Jack has received the ball. He pivots to face the basket, turning in just one movement. His opponent has no time to follow him.

TOP TACTICS

This move is called a fake and drive. It's useful for dribbling past tricky defenders. You pretend to go one way, then dodge the other way. Here's how it's done…

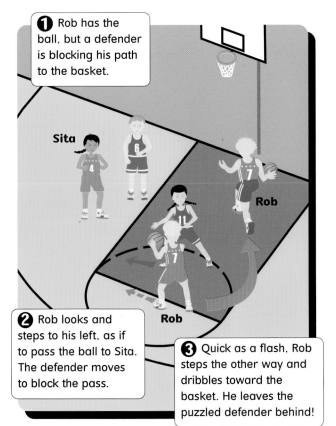

❶ Rob has the ball, but a defender is blocking his path to the basket.

❷ Rob looks and steps to his left, as if to pass the ball to Sita. The defender moves to block the pass.

❸ Quick as a flash, Rob steps the other way and dribbles toward the basket. He leaves the puzzled defender behind!

IN TRAINING!

Have a try with this drill — it will help you perfect your dribbling skills. Set up a row of imaginary defenders 2 yards (1.8 m) apart (cones are ideal, but you could use chairs or even T-shirts).

Dribble the ball around the obstacles. Practice with each hand and look straight ahead. Remember that you're not allowed to push your opponents during a game, so try not to bump into any of the imaginary defenders!

Passing

❝ Passing is the quickest way to move the ball, and it's crucial for good teamwork. Always be on the lookout for a chance to pass – you may be able to beat an opponent and give your teammate a chance to score. ❞

▲ Lisa Leslie of the USA prepares to pass to a teammate in a game against South Korea. Lisa is a top **WNBA** player.

Chest pass

A **chest pass** is simple and speedy, but it is easy for an opponent to **intercept**. So before you make this pass, check there are no defenders between you and your teammate.

1 Lucy holds the ball just below her chin. Her thumbs are behind the ball as she gets ready for this powerful pass.

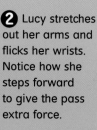

2 Lucy stretches out her arms and flicks her wrists. Notice how she steps forward to give the pass extra force.

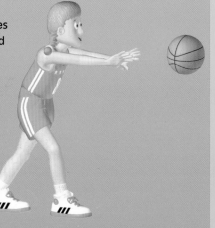

Overhead pass

Your opponent may try to block your pass. Why not pass the ball straight over his head? Don't throw the ball higher than you need to, but remember that your opponent will probably jump and try to win the ball.

Adam throws the ball with both hands toward Jack. He hopes the ball will sail right over the defender's head. Go for it, Adam!

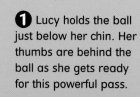

TOP TACTICS

If you can't go over, go around! A **bounce pass** is ideal for getting past an opponent whose arms are raised. Duck down quickly and throw the ball past the defender's legs! A bounce pass is slower than other passes, so use it only when your teammate is nearby.

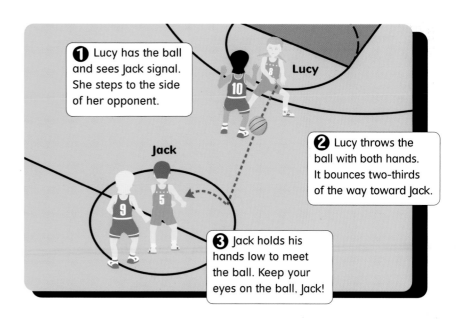

1 Lucy has the ball and sees Jack signal. She steps to the side of her opponent.

Lucy

Jack

2 Lucy throws the ball with both hands. It bounces two-thirds of the way toward Jack.

3 Jack holds his hands low to meet the ball. Keep your eyes on the ball, Jack!

Stopping

When you catch the ball in the air, you can take two steps; then you must stop moving. Try using either a jump stop, or a stride stop — these stops are also a good way to finish a **dribble**.

Jump stop
The best way to land is on both feet, because then you can **pivot** on either foot.

Stride stop
1 If you land on one foot this counts as your first step. You must keep this foot on the same spot.

2 Touch down with your other foot for your second step. Now pivot on your landing foot.

1st step   2nd step

IN TRAINING!

Play this game with two friends and you'll all brush up on your passing skills. Stand between your friends while they practice passing to each other. They should signal with their hands where they want to receive the ball.

Your job is to try to intercept their passes. When you've won the ball five times, change positions so that one of your friends is the one in the middle!

Shooting

66 Shooting is vital for **centers** like me, but everyone must be a smart shooter! At first, practice on your own, then try playing against a friend. Your shots won't all go in, but keep at it and you'll soon improve. **99**

▲ Hotshot player Shaquille O'Neal lines up a **free throw** for the USA during the 1996 Olympic Games.

Set shot

When you're standing still with the ball, near the basket, choose the **set shot**. This is also the shot to use when you take a free throw.

Adam is shooting with his right hand. He bends his knees and balances the ball with his left hand.

Adam stretches upward. He takes his left hand away from the ball and flicks the fingers of his right hand. It's a basket!

Layup shot

A **layup shot** is ideal when you're on the move with the ball. Shoot the ball the same way as you would for a set shot. Here's Lucy in action...

Lucy has caught the ball in mid-air, so she can take two steps. She lands on her left foot, then steps onto her right foot.

1st step
2nd step

Lucy pushes up off the ground with her right foot and shoots with her left hand.

Jump shot

A **jump shot** is a tricky shot to master, but it's also the most useful because it's difficult for an opponent to defend. Face the basket, bend your knees and leap straight upward off both feet. Keep your eyes fixed on the basket and release the ball just as you reach the top of your jump.

As Jack jumps, he lifts the ball with both hands above his head. Don't let the defenders put you off, Jack!

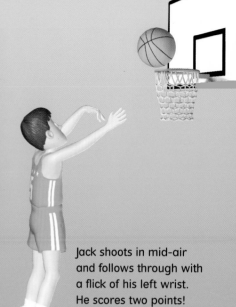

Jack shoots in mid-air and follows through with a flick of his left wrist. He scores two points!

▼ Karl Malone, a **forward** for Utah Jazz, reaches for the sky to score a superb layup shot. Karl's nickname is "the mailman" because he always delivers!

IN TRAINING!

For shooting practice, start near the basket and work on your set shots and jump shots. Once you've scored three baskets, take a step backward and try to score three more. Now move to the left and right of the basket.

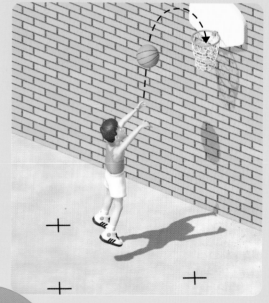

Practice with both your left hand and your right hand. Soon you'll be just as happy to shoot with either hand!

HOT TIPS
Every time you shoot, picture the ball going into the basket. Believe in yourself and you're more likely to score!

More shots

" Now let me show you the most exciting shots in the game. The great thing about the **hook shot** is that a defender finds it almost impossible to block. But you'll need to be amazing at jumping to pull off a **slam dunk!** "

▲ Kareem Abdul-Jabbar, of the Los Angeles Lakers, was a master of the hook shot from long range.

Hook shot

This shot takes time to perfect, but it will come in handy when you're facing away from the basket and there's a defender breathing down your neck. Here's how it's done…

1 Sita catches the ball and **pivots**. She needs to see the basket over her shoulder.

2 Sita looks over her shoulder at the basket and raises the ball to head-height.

3 She jumps and flips the ball toward the basket with her fingers. Watch how she raises her right knee for extra height.

HOT TIPS
Timing is crucial to successful **shooting**. Wait for the short pause at the top of your jump before you shoot.

4 Now Sita and her opponent face the basket and jostle for position in case the ball **rebounds**. Good work, Sita!

◀ The slam dunk is the most dramatic shot of all. Here's David Robinson of the San Antonio Spurs giving the fans a treat. David reaches above the **hoop** and pushes the ball down into the basket with both hands. What a winner!

WARNING
Don't try this shot on your own. Always make sure there's an adult or a coach nearby.

IN TRAINING!

You will need to work on your accuracy and timing to perfect the hook shot. This drill will help you to get going! Stand three steps away from the basket and shoot a hook shot. Move two steps sideways and shoot again. Then try from two steps to the other side. Once you have worked on your accuracy until you are really good, ask a friend to play as a defender. Try to score five times, then swap over so that you become the defender and your friend shoots.

Rebounds

66 Remember that lots of shots don't end up in the basket! When a shot bounces off the **hoop** or **backboard**, it's called a **rebound**. Your aim is to try to **block** your opponent and catch the rebound. Listen and I'll explain. 99

▲ Here, Dikembe Mutombo of the Atlanta Hawks defends his team's basket. He leaps to win a great rebound.

Blocking

Blocking (or boxing out) is basketball-speak for putting your body between your opponent and the basket. Being in the correct position is much more important than being tall!

As the ball hits the backboard, Jack stands right in front of his opponent, so that they are touching. Be careful not to foul her, Jack!

The ball rebounds and Jack explodes toward it. He catches the ball at the highest point of his jump.

DOs AND DON'Ts OF BLOCKING

There are a few things you'll need to remember when you're blocking an opponent...

Do...
● position yourself between your opponent and the basket, then turn to face the basket

● make body contact with your opponent

● follow your opponent wherever she goes

● watch the ball carefully and judge where it will fall.

Don't...
● stand too far away from your opponent – this gives her a chance to dodge around you and get closer to the basket

● jump before the ball has left the hoop or backboard

● push your opponent with your body or hands.

Attacking rebounds

Once you've reached a rebound, act quickly! If you're on the attack, now is your chance to try again for a basket. There are three ways you can do this. You can catch the ball and try a **jump shot** as soon as you've landed, or give these a try...

❶ If you're near the basket, you could try to tip the ball back in. Be warned – this is a difficult stunt to pull off!

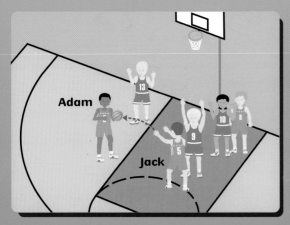

❷ If you're being **guarded** closely, pass the ball. Here, Jack has caught the rebound. In a split second, he passes to Adam. Now it's down to Adam to put the ball in the basket. Go for it!

TOP TACTICS

Catching a rebound is just as important when you're defending as when you're attacking. The aim is to move the ball at top speed to the other end of the **court**.

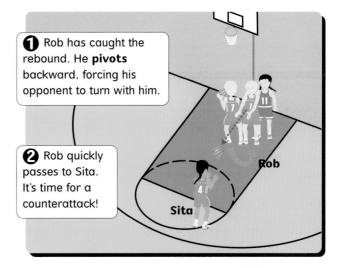

❶ Rob has caught the rebound. He **pivots** backward, forcing his opponent to turn with him.

❷ Rob quickly passes to Sita. It's time for a counterattack!

Rob

Sita

IN TRAINING!

Play this game to practice rebounding. Player 1 throws the ball against the backboard. Player 2 defends and tries to catch the ball, while player 3 attacks and tries to score.

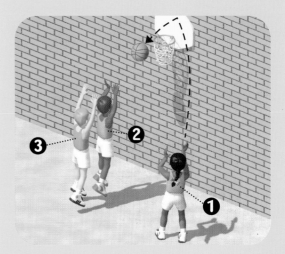

After five throws, swap around to play a different role. You win one point every time you catch the ball, and one point every time you score a basket.

Offense

" As soon as your team wins the ball, you're on **offense**. The aim is to move the ball quickly toward your opponents' basket. We call this 'breaking' down the **court**. Just give it a try and soon there'll be no stopping you! "

▲ Michael Jordan was deadly on offense. His lightning pace helped him score thousands of baskets in the **NBA**.

Fast break

A fast break is any team's most important offensive move. The minute you win the ball, race as fast as you can down the court, before your opponents have the chance to run back and defend. Quick passing and sharp **dribbling** will help you to outrun the defenders and go straight for the basket.

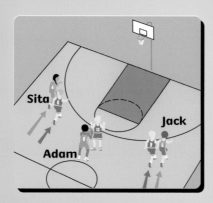

The red team is making a fast break and Adam has the ball. As Sita and Jack sprint forward, Sita signals to Adam to pass to her.

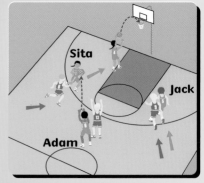

Adam throws the ball ahead of Sita and she catches it on the move. Sita dribbles forward, then scores with a **layup shot**. Nice work, team!

Backdoor

When you want a teammate to pass to you but your opponent is blocking the way, try a sneaky backdoor move. To fool your opponent, step toward your teammate and signal for the ball. Then run toward the basket. If you're quick enough, you'll be able to outsmart your opponent.

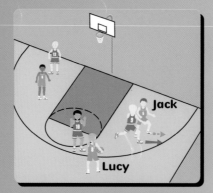

Lucy can't pass to Jack because a defender is in the way. So Jack fakes a step to his left. The defender falls for the trick and moves with him.

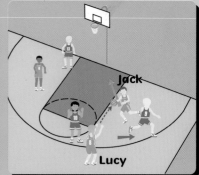

Jack sprints to the basket, away from both Lucy and the defender. He signals again, and Lucy passes to him. Now go for a shot, Jack!

TOP TACTICS

This move is called the give and go, and you do just that. Give (pass) the ball to a teammate, then go (sprint) to the basket. Your teammate passes the ball back to you, giving you a chance to score a basket.

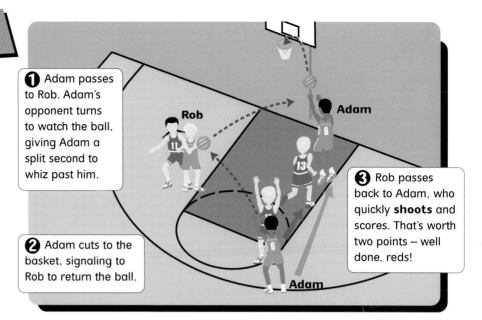

1 Adam passes to Rob. Adam's opponent turns to watch the ball, giving Adam a split second to whiz past him.

Rob

Adam

3 Rob passes back to Adam, who quickly **shoots** and scores. That's worth two points — well done, reds!

2 Adam cuts to the basket, signaling to Rob to return the ball.

Adam

IN TRAINING!

Here's a team game for four players that will help you polish up your offensive tactics. The green team goes on offense and tries to score as many baskets as possible. The red team tries to stop the greens from scoring.

When the reds win the ball, they must give it back to the greens. After five minutes, the teams swap roles. The winner is the team with the most baskets!

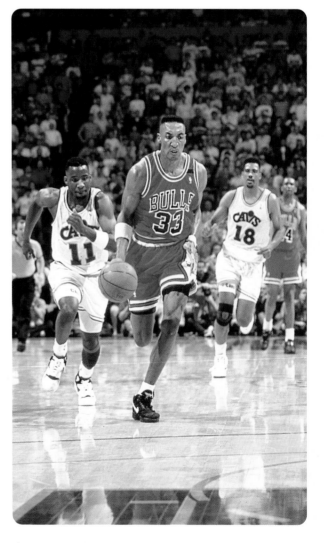

▲ Scottie Pippen has won two Olympic gold medals with the USA. Here, he speeds away on a superb fast break for the Chicago Bulls.

Defense

" You may know how to win points, but if your team doesn't defend well, you'll never win! I'm a **guard** and we're especially good at defending, but it's up to every team member to keep the opposition away from your basket. "

▲ Tim Duncan of the San Antonio Spurs defends expertly to put shooter Kevin Garnett under pressure.

Defending against a passer

When your opponent wants to pass the ball, position yourself between her and the basket. Try to prevent the pass by blocking the path of the ball with your hands. Keep your feet moving and stay alert!

Rob stands in front of the passer and waves his arms around to distract her. His knees are bent and his fingers are spread out.

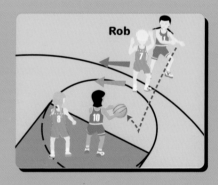

Rob's opponent makes the pass, but Rob doesn't follow the ball. Instead, he stays with his opponent in case the ball is passed back again.

Defending against a dribbler

You need quick reactions to stop your opponent from **dribbling** around you. Try to judge which way the dribbler will go — you'll find this easier if you don't get too close. Your feet should be flat on the floor so that you stay well balanced.

Lucy shuffles sideways, moving with her opponent. As the dribbler tries to move away, Lucy follows him and quickly blocks his path.

Lucy moves closer to her opponent and tries to flick the ball away with her left hand. Be careful not to make body contact with the dribbler, Lucy!

TOP TACTICS

There are several different ways to defend. The easiest is called man-to-man **defense**. As soon as the green team wins the ball, each red player moves into position to guard one attacker.

1 Rob guards the player with the ball. He faces his opponent and moves toward her.

2 Every other red player stands a little further away from his or her opponent.

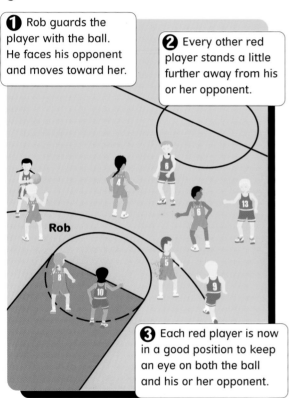

Rob

3 Each red player is now in a good position to keep an eye on both the ball and his or her opponent.

HOT TIPS
Don't forget the time rules! If you can make your opponent hold on to the ball for five seconds, your team wins the ball.

▲ Dennis Rodman, playing for the Chicago Bulls, spreads out his arms and legs and does an excellent job of guarding his opponent, John Stockton.

IN TRAINING!

Solid footwork is vital for good defense. Try this to improve your footwork! Chalk a zigzag line on the ground, then ask a friend to dribble up and down along the line. It's your job to mark the dribbler by moving with him, parallel to the zigzag line. Shuffle your feet sideways along the floor, but don't bring them together or cross them at any time. Keep practicing until you can beat the dribbler to the end of the line. Then swap roles with your friend.

Advanced play

" Now you've got the hang of basic basketball skills, let's try something more tricky. These moves are not easy, but, as any basketball hero will tell you, hard work and dedication are the secrets of success! "

▲ Magic Johnson controls the ball excellently as he **dribbles** behind his back – while in mid-air!

Fancy dribbling

Dribbling the ball through your legs is a handy way to outwit your opponent – and it looks great, too. Simply bounce the ball with one hand and catch it with the other. First, practice this technique on the spot, then try it while you're on the move.

Sita stands with her legs apart. She dribbles the ball around her legs in a figure of eight, passing the ball from one hand to the other.

Now Sita is on the move. As she steps forward with her left foot, she bounces the ball through her legs from her right hand to her left.

Fancy passing

Catch your opponent off-guard with a sneaky pass behind your back. First, practice moving the ball in a circle around your waist, passing the ball from one hand to the other. Then use this technique to pass to a friend during a game. Here's Rob in action…

As Rob finishes his dribble, he takes the ball behind his back with his left hand. Don't take more than two steps with the ball, Rob.

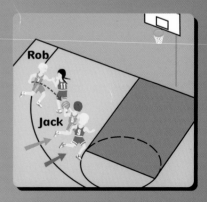

Rob lets the ball roll off his fingertips and flicks it towards Jack. Nice work, Rob – the green defenders weren't expecting that!

Screening

When your teammate has the ball and defenders are **guarding** you both closely, try this move, called a screen. Block, or screen, the player guarding your teammate, leaving your teammate free to pass or dribble the ball.

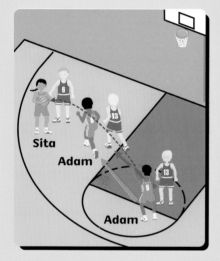

Adam passes to Sita, then runs to position himself next to Sita's opponent. The player guarding Adam follows him in case Sita returns the pass.

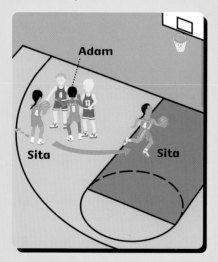

Sita steps to her left to fool the defenders, then she dribbles to the right. Her opponent tries to follow her, but is blocked, or screened, by Adam.

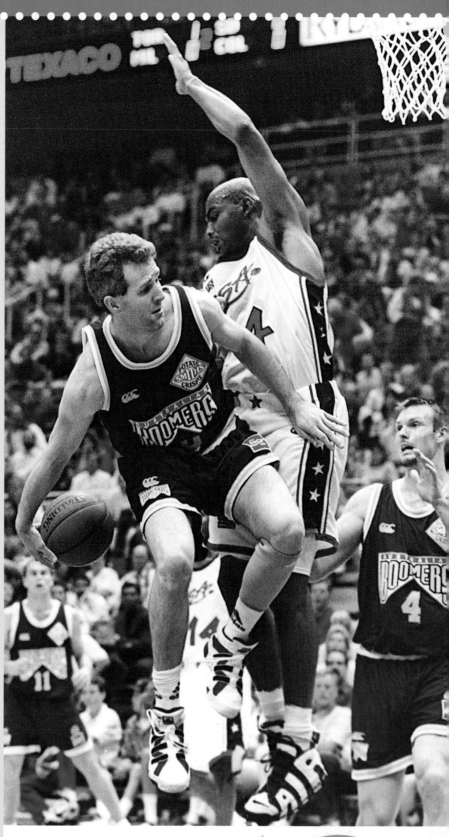

▲ Andrew Gaze is one of Australia's top players. Here, he shows off his expert skills in a clash with Charles Barkley of the USA. Andrew coolly passes the ball behind his back to his teammate, in the number '4' shirt.

HOT TIPS
When you pass behind your back, try to look straight ahead so that your opponent doesn't suspect anything!

Hall of Fame

" There are lots of great basketball players out there, but only a handful go down in history as the best in the business. The stars here have done just that — I think they're among the most exciting players of all time. "

HOT SHOTS
In international basketball, the USA are way ahead. They've won gold medals at 11 out of the last 14 Olympic Games.

TERESA EDWARDS

Name Teresa Edwards
Date of birth July 19, 1964
Height 5 ft 11 in (1 m 80 cm)
NBA teams Atlanta Glory

Did you know? Teresa is the first US basketball player to enter four Olympics. She won three gold medals and one bronze.
Achievements Top player Teresa is head coach to Atlanta Glory, and the ABL's record holder for points in a single game (46). She has twice been named USA Basketball Athlete of the Year, in 1987 and 1990.

MICHAEL JORDAN

Name Michael Jeffrey Jordan
Date of birth February 17, 1963
Height 6 ft 6 in (1 m 98 cm)
NBA team Chicago Bulls

Did you know? Michael was dropped from his high school basketball team. The coaches thought he was too small and not good enough to play!
Achievements Michael is probably the greatest-ever basketball player. He has been named **NBA** Most Valuable Player five times, and has won two Olympic gold medals. During the 1990s, he helped the Chicago Bulls win the NBA championship an amazing six times.

MAGIC JOHNSON

Name Earvin Johnson Jr. — but better known by his nickname, Magic!
Date of birth August 14, 1959
Height 6 ft 9 in (2 m 6 cm)
NBA team Los Angeles Lakers

Did you know? Magic is a major television celebrity. He has even starred in *The Simpsons*!
Achievements Magic was one of the greatest passers of the ball. In 1980, during his first season in the NBA, Magic helped his team win the championship. Later, he went on to win a gold medal at the 1992 Olympic Games.

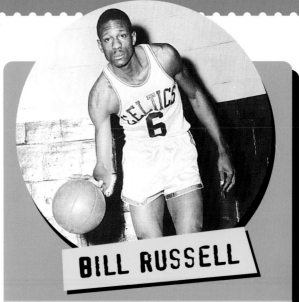

BILL RUSSELL

Name William Felton Russell
Date of birth February 12, 1934
Height 6 ft 10 in (2 m 8 cm)
NBA team Boston Celtics

Did you know? Bill was an outstanding high-jumper. His best jump, of 8.5 ft (2.6 m), nearly broke the world record.
Achievements Bill led the Boston Celtics to the NBA championship title no less than 11 times! He won an Olympic gold medal in 1956, and later became the first black NBA head coach, with his old team, the Celtics.

LARRY BIRD

Name Larry Joe Bird
Date of birth December 7, 1956
Height 6 ft 9 in (2 m 6 cm)
NBA team Boston Celtics

Did you know? The people of Boston are so proud of Larry that they have named a street after him.
Achievements Larry has won a host of honors, including an Olympic gold medal in 1992. He was the NBA Most Valuable Player for three years running — only the third player to achieve this feat. Larry could score **three-pointers** with his eyes closed. What a shooting star!

Basketball buzzwords

backboard The flat board behind the basket.

back court The half of the court that your team defends.

blocking Standing between your opponent and the basket to try to win a rebound. This is also known as boxing out.

bounce pass A pass in which you bounce the ball off the floor toward a teammate.

center A playing position, or a player who usually scores from close range.

chest pass A short, direct pass made at chest height.

court A marked area where a game is played. A regulation court is 94 ft (28.7 m) long and 50 ft (15.2 m) wide. A high school court may be 84 ft (25.6 m) long.

defense When your opponents have the ball, your team is on defense. You must protect your basket and try to stop your opponents from scoring.

dribbling Moving around the court while bouncing the ball.

FIBA This stands for the Fédération Internationale de Basketball. FIBA organizes the rules and competitions for international basketball. Some FIBA rules are slightly different from US college and NBA rules.

forward A playing position, or a player who usually scores from the sides of the court.

foul If you unfairly hinder another player, you commit a foul. A personal foul usually involves holding or pushing another player. A technical foul is given for bad or unsporting behavior.

free throw If an opponent fouls you while you are shooting, the Ref will award you up to three free shots from the free-throw line.

free-throw lane The part of the court in front of the basket, from the end line to the free-throw line. It is also known as the foul lane.

front court The half of the court that your team attacks.

guard A playing position, or a player who starts attacking moves and shoots from long range.

hook shot A shot in which you face away from the basket, pivot, and flip the ball over your head.

hoop The metal ring that holds the basket net.

intercepting Stepping in and stealing a ball that your opponent has thrown towards a teammate.

jump ball Each period of a game begins with a jump ball. The Ref throws the ball up and one player from each team tries to tap it to a teammate. A jump ball to start the game is called a tip-off.

jump shot A shot in which you jump straight upward off both feet.

layup shot A shot that you take while you are on the move.

man-to-man defense A system of defense in which each player guards an opponent to stop him or her passing or receiving the ball.

NBA This stands for the National Basketball Association. The NBA runs men's professional basketball in the USA.

NBA game An NBA game usually lasts for 48 minutes, with a one-and-a-half minute break between quarters and a 15-minute break in the middle.

offense When your team has the ball, you are on offense. Try to move past your opponents and shoot at the basket.

out-of-bounds Outside the boundary lines of the court.

overhead pass A pass in which you throw the ball over your opponent's head.

pivoting Turning on the spot, either with small steps, or in one try, while keeping one foot fixed and holding onto the ball.

rebound A shot that misses the basket and bounces off the hoop or backboard.

referee The referee, or Ref, makes sure that the players stick to the rules. If they don't, the Ref gives the ball to the other team for a free throw or a throw-in.

set shot A shot that you take near the basket, with both feet on the floor.

shooting Trying to throw the ball into the basket to score points.

slam dunk A shot in which you jump, reach above the hoop, then push the ball down into the basket.

three-pointer A goal scored from behind the three-point line, and worth three points.

throw-in A throw from outside the sidelines or end lines. This is also known as sideline or end-line possession.

time out A break in play for the coach to discuss tactics with his players. Each team can take up to five time outs in a college game. The teams are also allowed one additional time out for each overtime period.

triple-threat position A way of standing and holding the ball which gives you three options – to dribble, pass, or shoot.

violation When you break a rule, except when you commit a foul, this is called a violation. The Ref awards the ball to the other team.

WNBA This stands for the Women's National Basketball Association, which runs women's professional basketball in the USA.

zone defense A system of defense in which each player guards a certain area of the court. Zone defense is not allowed in NBA games.

Index

What next?

So you want to know more about playing basketball? Here are a few hot tips…

● First talk to your PE teacher and find out if there's a school team that you can join.

● Look out for details of courses and basketball camps at your local library or YMCA.

● Train as often as you can, and try to get plenty of game experience. With hard work and dedication, you may win a place in your school or local team. Good luck!

Useful addresses

NBA
645 5th Ave, 10th floor
New York, NY 10022
Telephone:
(212) 407 8000

WNBA
645 5th Ave,
10th floor
New York, NY 10022
Telephone:
(212) 688 9622